Revised and updated in 2021 by Wayland
First published in 2003 by Wayland
Text copyright © Pat Thomas 2003
Illustrations copyright © Lesley Harker 2003

Wayland, an imprint of Hachette Children's Group
Part of Hodder and Stoughton
Carmelite House
50 Victoria Embankment
London EC4Y 0DZ

An Hachette UK Company
www.hachette.co.uk

Printed and bound in China

Concept design: Sarah Finan
Series design: Paul Cherrill Creative Design

PB ISBN: 9781526317605
EBK ISBN: 9781526319326

Every effort has been made by the Publishers
to ensure that the websites in this book
contain no inappropriate or offensive
material. However, because of the nature of
the Internet, it is impossible to guarantee that
the contents of these sites will not be altered.

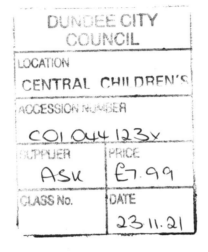

C01 044 123Y

Return
Please
Items
reque

MY AMAZING BODY

A FIRST LOOK AT HEALTH AND FITNESS

Written by
PAT THOMAS

Illustrated by
LESLEY HARKER

WAYLAND

You have an amazing body.

So do all the other people in the world.

You have a brain that can do more complicated thinking than any computer.

You have a body that can move in more different ways than any robot.

You have five senses — sight, hearing, taste, touch, and smell — that tell you lots of important things about the world around you, without you even having to ask.

Your body can do lots of other things on its own,
too. Your heart beats, your lungs breathe –

and when you graze your knee or get a cold,
your body can make you well again.

But your body can't do
everything on its own.
It needs some help
from you.

There are lots of ways you can help your body to stay fit and healthy. All of them are easy and most of them are fun as well.

WHAT ABOUT YOU?

How many different things can you think of that help keep your body healthy? How often do you do these things?

Food contains vitamins, minerals and energy. These things help you to think and play and grow.

When you eat fresh fruits and vegetables and protein foods, such as meat, milk and beans, you are giving your body the things it needs to grow.

But when you eat lots
of sweets, chips and
soft drinks you are
not giving your
body the vitamins
it needs.

These foods and drinks may taste nice, but if you have them too often your body may become sick.

It's okay to eat these foods sometimes.
But the best way to stay healthy is to eat lots
of different kinds of foods every day.

Another way to help your body is to use it in every way you can. That means getting lots of exercise. Exercise helps your muscles stay strong and fit and helps your bones grow.

When you are running and jumping and stretching,
you are exercising your heart and helping it to pump blood
all over your body. You are also exercising your lungs,
helping them to breathe in more air.

WHAT ABOUT YOU?

What are your favourite types of
exercise? How often do you get
to do these things?

There are other good ways
to help your body
stay healthy.

When you bathe and brush your teeth you are
helping keep yourself clean and free from germs.

And while exercising is good, resting is important, too.

We all need plenty of sleep and to have times when we can work or play quietly.

Your body is always giving you clues about what it needs. When your body needs rest, you feel tired.

When your body needs food, you feel hungry.

And when your body has had enough food, you feel full.

When you feel a pain it's
a message that a part of you
needs care and attention.
It's important to listen to the
messages your body
is sending you.

Even healthy people get ill sometimes. It's never fun to get sick, but when you are sick your body is doing something amazing.

It is making a memory of that illness, so that next time you can get better more quickly.

You only have one body and it is the most important thing you will ever own.

Your body is built
to last you a long time. And if
you take really good care of it, it will.

HOW TO USE THIS BOOK

Children often imitate adults when it comes to eating habits. If parents are rarely seen eating fresh fruits and vegetables or freshly prepared meals, children will learn that this is the correct way to eat. Prepackaged foods are convenient but are often nutritionally poor. As often as is practical, parents should strive to put fresh food on the table. Likewise, children usually copy their parents' exercise habits. To encourage your child to get up and move, you may have to do the same. Special activities for children, such as Saturday football or swimming, are great. But regular activities that all the family can enjoy are also a good way of encouraging your child to be active.

There is an argument that, for small children, several small meals throughout the day is a better way to maintain health and absorb nutrients since it places less stress on the digestive system. While there is a place in most diets for crackers and candy, these need to be balanced by healthier alternatives. A well-chosen snack can also ward off the extreme hunger that can lead to continual cravings and bingeing on the wrong kinds of foods. Often children will eat whatever is around, so it's best to make sure there is always a bowl of colourful fruit on hand for children to choose from.

Food fads and a decreased appetite are normal during childhood. As your child's growth slows down, appetite will also decline. Although it may seem that your child is not eating enough, it is highly unlikely that your child's appetite will decrease to such an extent that health is compromised. At some point during the pre-school years, many children go through another growth spurt. Take advantage of your child's increased appetite at this time and introduce a greater variety of healthier food options based on freshly prepared dishes and unprocessed whole foods.

Schools may be well suited to teach about diet and fitness from many different angles. Exploring different religious customs that involve food or finding out about the foods people from other cultures eat can broaden children's horizons considerably.

Similarly, introducing a wide range of physical education or playground activities can aid children in finding a sport that suits them.

Some schools have found that introducing a 'snack time' in the afternoon is influential. Once children leave preschool they often don't have an afternoon break of this nature. A ten-minute break in the afternoon for the class to snack on healthy foods can improve energy levels and help to reinforce good eating habits.

GLOSSARY

energy Energy is the fuel that makes your body work properly. Your food provides the energy that powers your brain, your muscles, and all the other parts of your body.

germs Germs are living things that are too small to see. They don't usually cause problems to you. If you are not strong because you are eating the wrong foods or not getting enough sleep, then it is possible that the germs could cause you to become sick.

nutrients The vitamins and minerals in your food are known as nutrients. These are the things your body needs to grow and stay healthy.

WEBSITES

www.healthforkids.co.uk/

https://www.nhs.uk/change4life

www.nutrition.gov/topics/nutrition-age/children/kids-corner

https://kidshealth.org/en/parents/habits.html

https://healthy-kids.com.au/food-nutrition/

FURTHER READING

Healthy Me: Exercise and Fitness/Eating Well
by Katie Woolley and Ryan Wheatcroft
(Wayland, 2018)

I Care About My Body
by Liz Lennon
(Franklin Watts, 2021)

Me and My World: Growing Body
by C.J.Polin and Ryan Wheatcroft
(Franklin Watts, 2021)

Oliver's Fruit Salad
by Vivian French
(Orchard Books, 1998)

Pooh's Little Fitness Book
by A. A. Milne
(Dutton, 1996)

The Very Hungry Caterpillar
by Eric Carle
(Penguin, 1994)

Why Do I Have to: Go to Sleep?/Eat Well?/Keep Clean?
by Kay Barnham and Patrick Corrigan
(Franklin Watts, 2021)

Your Body and You
by Anita Ganeri
(Franklin Watts, 2021)